# Mom! Dad! What Should I Do?

Written by Allen Green
Illustrated by Kenady Kitchen

# Mom! Dad! What Should I Do?

Written By Allen Green

Illustrated by Kenady Kitchen

Copyright © 2024 by Allen Green

All rights reserved. This book or parts thereof may not be reproduced in any form, stored in any retrieval system, or transmitted in any form by any means—electronic, mechanical, photocopy, recording, or otherwise—without prior written permission of the publisher, except as provided by United States of America copyright law or for the use of brief quotations in a book review.

This is a work of fiction. Names, characters, businesses, places, events and incidents are either the products of the author's imagination or used in a fictitious manner. Any resemblance to actual persons, living or dead, or actual events is purely coincidental.

Cover Illustration Copyright © 2024 by Kenady Kitchen
**Printed in the United States of America**
**First Printing, 2024**
**ISBN : 978-1-68598-028-3**
**Write Womb Ink**
**Chattanooga, TN 37411**

## To inquire about bulk orders or speaking engagement, please contact Allen Green allengreen23@yahoo.com

# WHEN THERE IS AN EMERGENCY

 ## CALL 911

## My Home Address Is

_____

_____

"GOOD MORNING, MY WONDERFUL STUDENTS! WOULD ANYBODY LIKE TO SHARE SOMETHING ABOUT THEIR WEEKEND WITH THE CLASS?" ASKED MS. ROBERTS.

MARIA SLOWLY RAISED HER HAND.
"ALL RIGHT! LET'S HEAR IT, MARIA."

"MY DAD CAUSED A SMALL FIRE IN THE KITCHEN ON SATURDAY MORNING WHILE COOKING BREAKFAST. ALL THE SMOKE ALARMS WENT OFF FROM THE SMOKE THAT QUICKLY FILLED THE KITCHEN. IT SEEMED LIKE THE WHOLE FIRE DEPARTMENT CAME TO OUR HOUSE."

"MY MOM AND I WENT OUTSIDE TO OUR MEETING PLACE WHILE DAD PUT THE SMALL FIRE OUT WITH THE KITCHEN FIRE EXTINGUISHER. DAD MET US AT THE MAILBOX, AND WE WAITED FOR THE FIRE DEPARTMENT."

"WHAT IS A MEETING PLACE?" WHISPERED JACOB, MARIA'S BEST FRIEND.

MARIA REPLIED, "IT'S A SAFE PLACE OUTSIDE THE HOUSE WHERE MY FAMILY MEETS IF THERE IS A FIRE EMERGENCY IN OUR HOUSE. YOU SHOULD GO HOME AND ASK YOUR PARENTS ABOUT YOUR MEETING PLACE!"

Jacob burst through the door, with excitement to share Maria's story with his family. "Mom! Dad!" he exclaimed, "If there's a fire in the house, what's our escape plan? Where's our secret family meeting space?"

"COME SIT WITH ME, JACOB," SAID DAD.

JACOB AND DAD SAT DOWN AT THE KITCHEN TABLE. "COME ON MOM," SAID JACOB.

DAD PULLED OUT A BIG SHEET OF PAPER AND DREW A MAP OF THE INSIDE OF THEIR HOME.

THE MAP INCLUDED EACH LEVEL OF THE HOME AND ALL DOORS AND WINDOWS. DAD CIRCLED THE INITIALS "SA" FOR THE LOCATION OF THE SMOKE ALARMS. DAD EXPLAINED THAT THE MAP NEEDS TO HAVE A LAYOUT OF THE HOME AND SHOW ALL WINDOWS AND DOORS. WHILE POINTING TO THE WINDOWS AND DOORS IN THE HOUSE, DAD SAID, "JACOB, YOU SHOULD KNOW AT LEAST TWO WAYS OUT OF EVERY ROOM. DAD MARKED TWO WAYS OUT OF EACH ROOM ON THE MAP.

"WE MUST ALSO HAVE A SAFE PLACE TO MEET ONCE WE GET OUTSIDE.

JACOB ASKED, "WHERE IS OUR MEETING PLACE?"

DAD SAID, "OUR MEETING PLACE WILL BE AT OUR MAILBOX.

GO THERE AND WAIT FOR MOM AND ME.

CALL 911 IF YOU CAN, AND NEVER GO BACK INSIDE THE HOUSE."

"GET OUT AND STAY OUT! THIS IS OUR FAMILY ESCAPE PLAN TO GET OUT OF THE HOUSE SAFELY IF THERE IS A FIRE. WE WILL PRACTICE THIS PLAN AT LEAST TWICE A YEAR DURING DAYTIME AND NIGHTTIME."

Dad said, "Jacob, I have a question for you now." Jacob looked puzzled. "Do you know our home address? You need to know this so the firefighters can find our location quickly."

"Dad, I don't know our address. Can you teach me?"

"I sure will," replied Dad.

"THANK YOU, DAD!" SAID JACOB. "I CAN'T WAIT TO SHARE WITH MY CLASS TOMORROW WHAT I LEARNED ABOUT FIRE SAFETY AND OUR FAMILY ESCAPE PLAN."

THE NEXT DAY AT SCHOOL, JACOB SHARED WITH HIS CLASS WHAT HE HAD LEARNED AND WHAT THEY SHOULD DO DURING A FIRE EMERGENCY.

# HOME FIRE SAFETY QUESTIONS

WHAT SHOULD YOU DO IF YOU SEE SMOKE OR FLAMES IN YOUR HOUSE?

DOES YOUR FAMILY HAVE A HOME FIRE ESCAPE PLAN?

WHY IS IT IMPORTANT TO HAVE AN ESCAPE PLAN FOR YOUR HOUSE?

WHERE IS YOUR FAMILY MEETING PLACE?

WHY IS IT IMPORTANT TO HAVE A FAMILY MEETING PLACE?

# HOME FIRE SAFETY QUESTIONS

SHOULD YOU EVER GO BACK INSIDE THE HOUSE ONCE YOU GET OUT?

DOES YOUR FAMILY HAVE WORKING SMOKE ALARMS?

WHAT SHOULD YOU DO IF YOUR CLOTHES CATCH ON FIRE?

WHAT IS THE PHONE NUMBER TO DIAL DURING AN EMERGENCY?

DO YOU KNOW YOUR ADDRESS?

# HOME FIRE SAFETY MAP
## CREATE YOUR OWN FIRE ESCAPE MAP FOR EACH FLOOR OF YOUR HOME

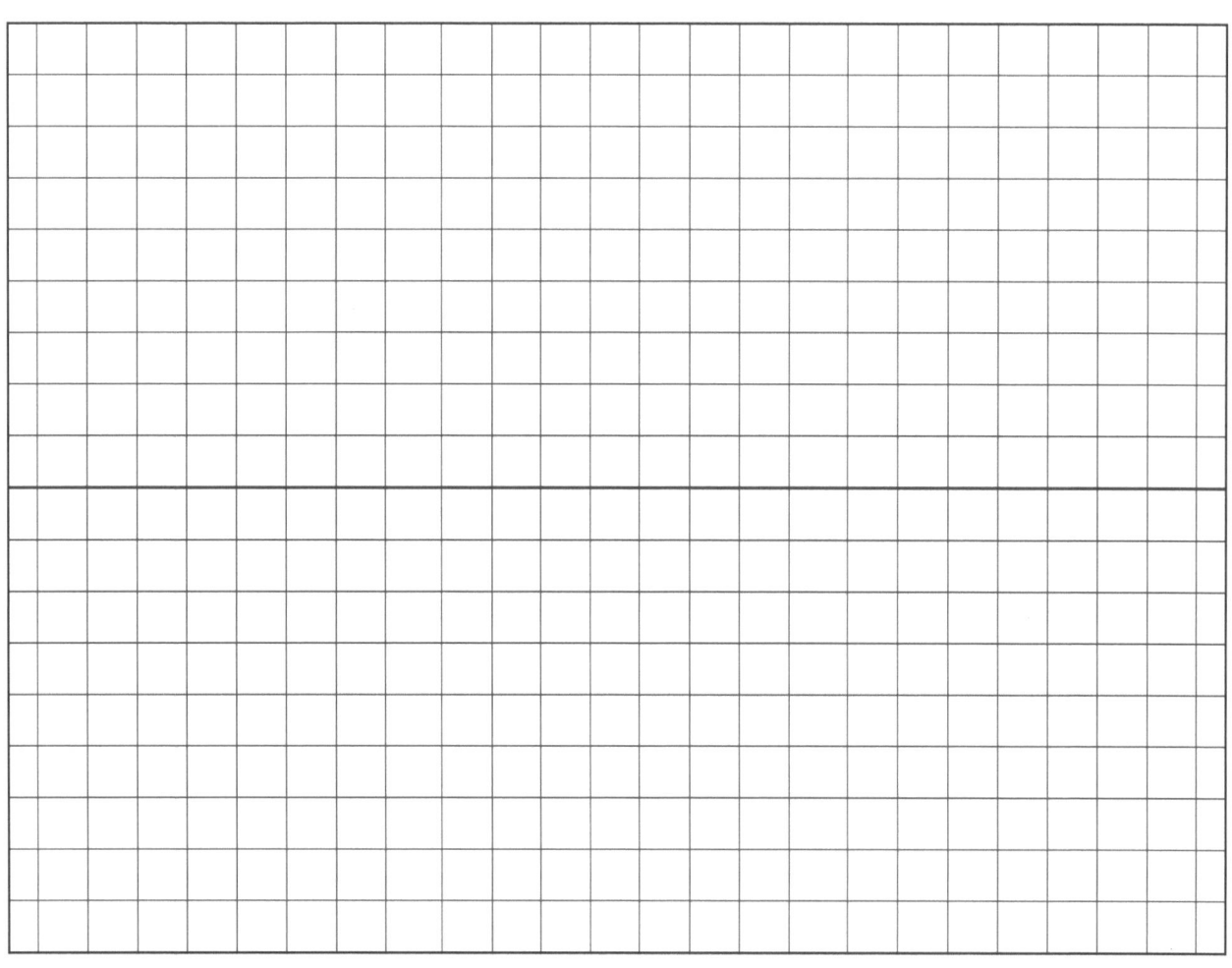

# HOME FIRE SAFETY MAP

CREATE YOUR OWN FIRE ESCAPE MAP FOR EACH FLOOR OF YOUR HOME

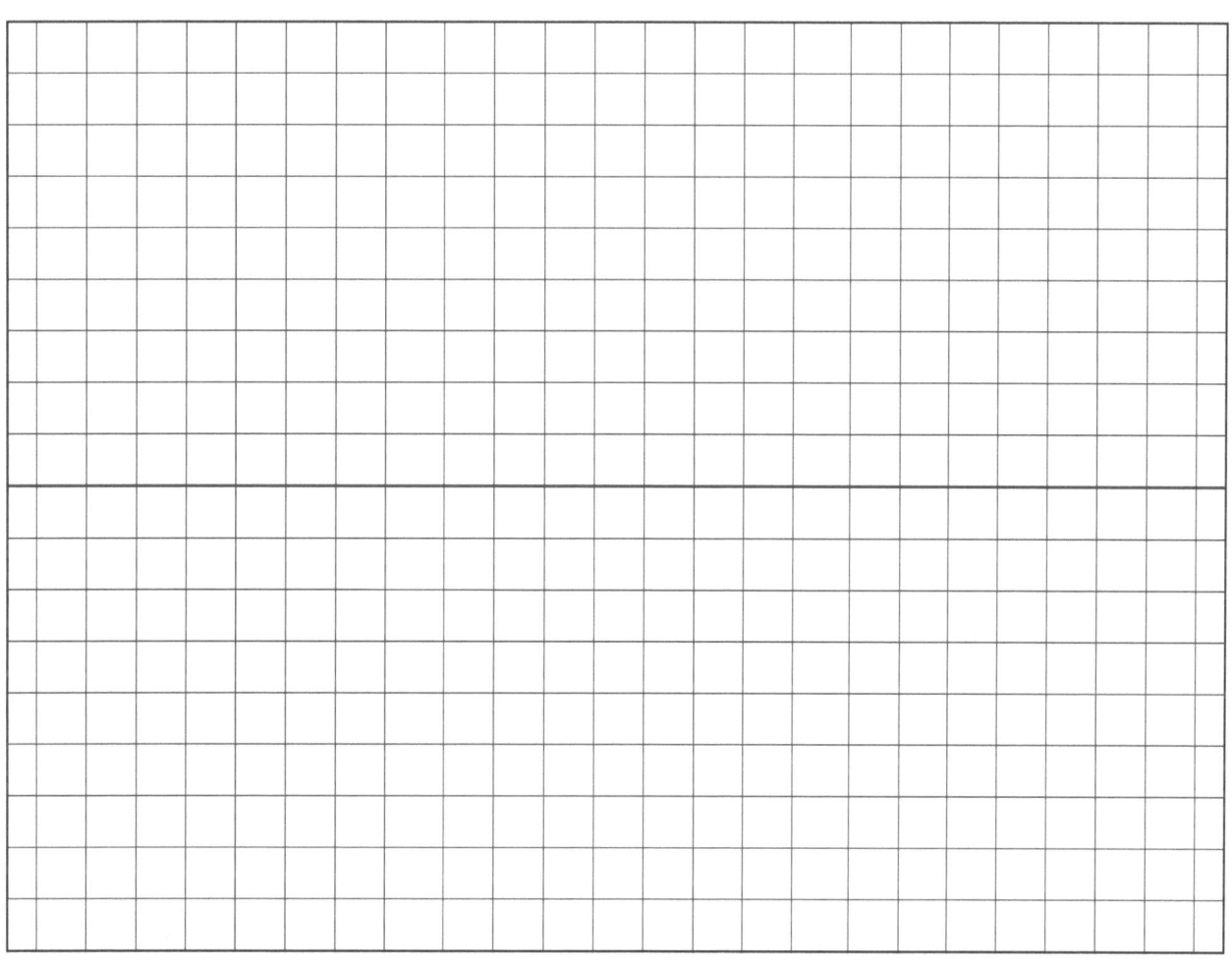

# HOME FIRE SAFETY MAP
## CREATE YOUR OWN FIRE ESCAPE MAP FOR EACH FLOOR OF YOUR HOME

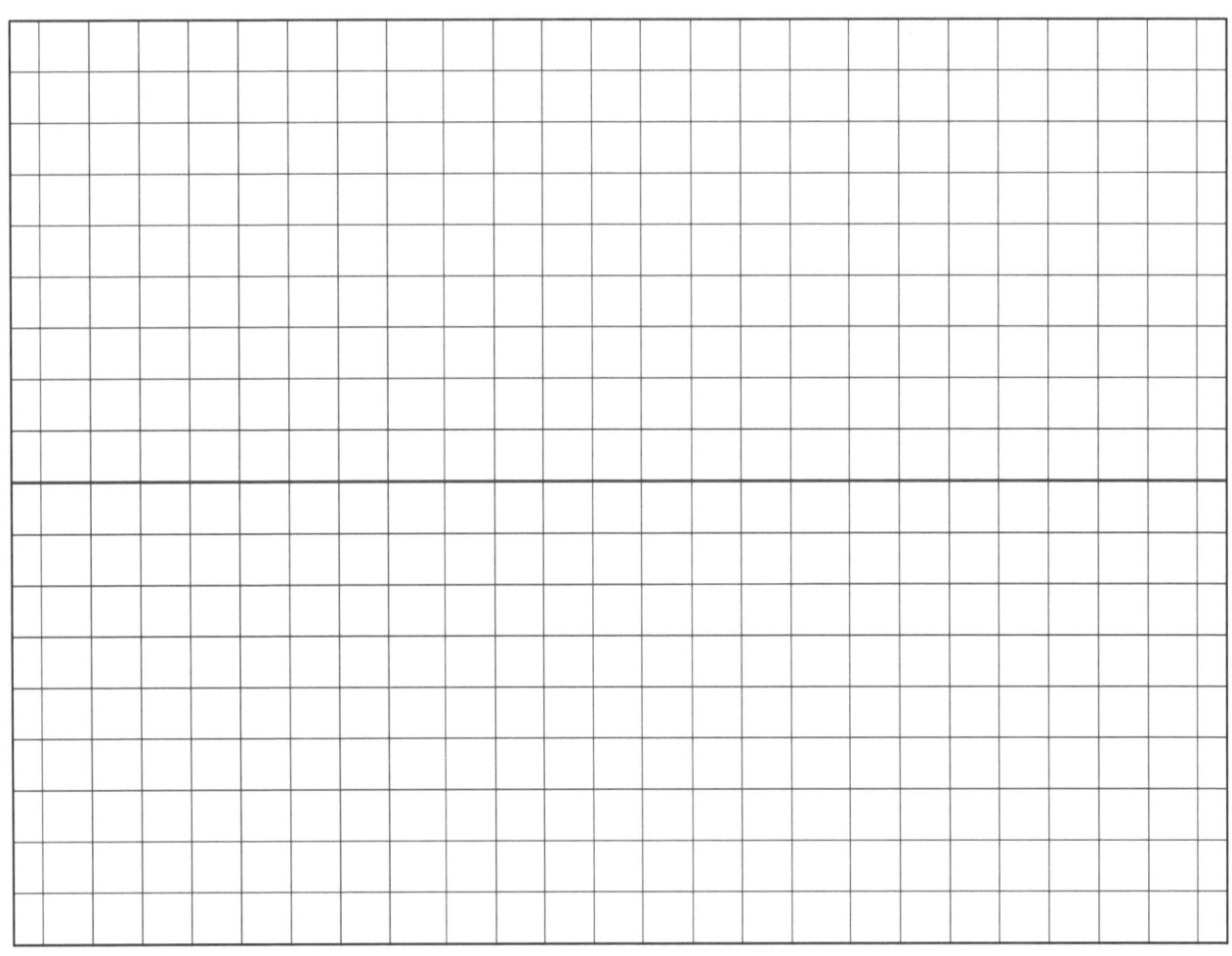

# HOME FIRE SAFETY MAP

CREATE YOUR OWN FIRE ESCAPE MAP FOR EACH FLOOR OF YOUR HOME

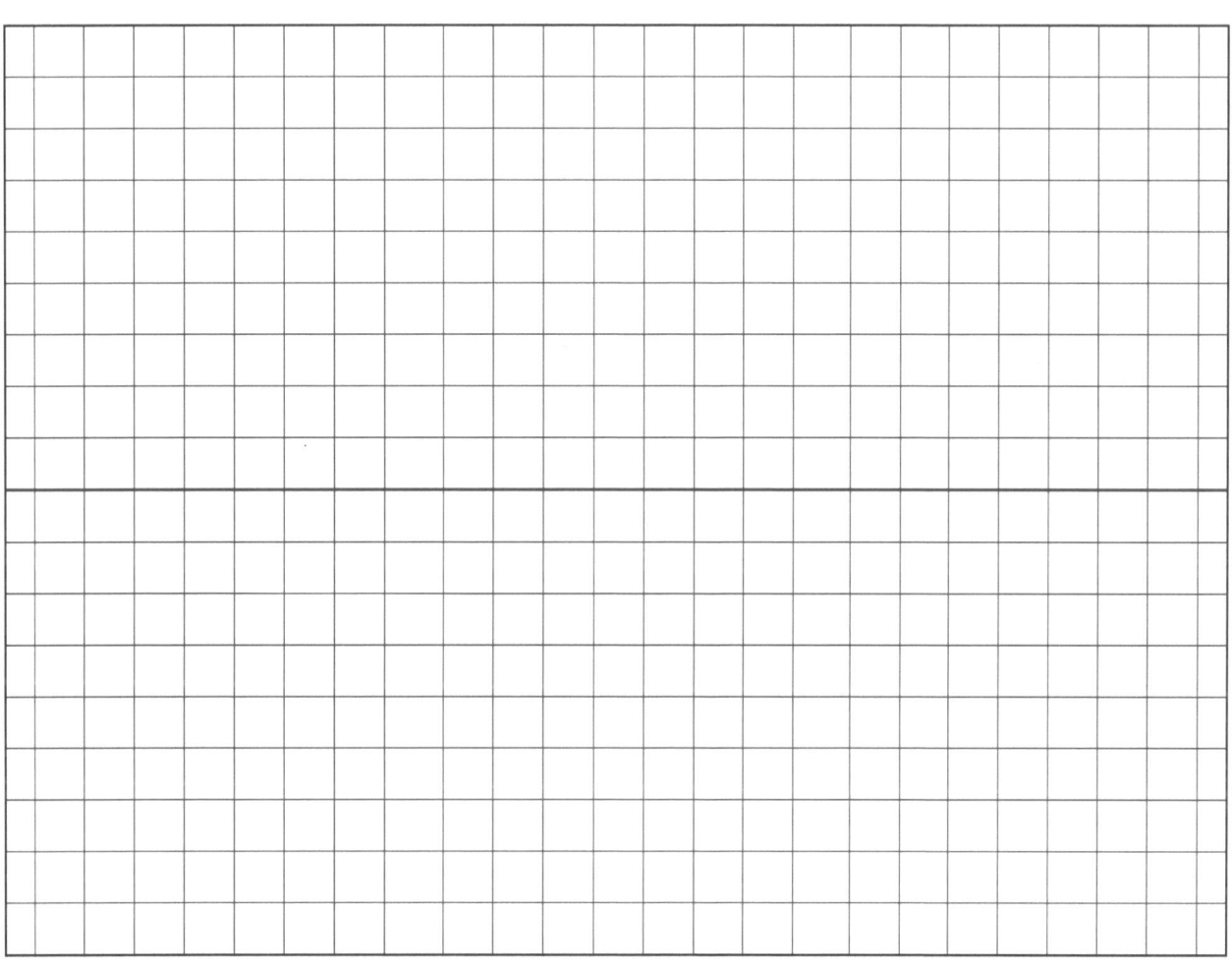

# HELP JACOB FIND HIS WAY TO THE MAILBOX!!

# HELP THE FIRETRUCK SAVE THE BURNING HOUSE!

# Word Search

```
I O H G D E S C A P E I X L Z
M A I L B O X Q U E O Y G X Y
C B F W L V S M N M A Q Z I I
W S F I I Q X A Z X L V B Q N
Z A W A R N U P D R A S Y Q F
D F U M C E D J Q S R M E A I
J E J E E E D O A X M O M D R
N T D E S O P A W C O K E D E
B Y O T Q R Y H N S O E R R F
J Y O I D Y J A O G V B G E I
T H R N I I M L F N E Q E S G
G F B G R P W A Q Y E R N S H
J N M Q Z L P Y R U H F C D T
Q H T O E A F N J I L O Y O E
G X I V F N L N V E A C Y C R
```

| | | | |
|---|---|---|---|
| firefighter | emergency | meeting | fire |
| windows | mailbox | address | plan |
| escape | danger | smoke | door |
| Jacob | safety | phone | map |
| Maria | alarm | | |

24

## ABOUT THE AUTHOR

ALLEN GREEN WAS BORN AND RAISED IN CHATTANOOGA. HE GRADUATED FROM THE UNIVERSITY OF TENNESSEE AT CHATTANOOGA WITH A DEGREE IN CHEMISTRY AND A MINOR IN BIOLOGY. ALLEN SERVES AS A FIRE AND LIFE SAFETY EDUCATOR AND IS ALSO A YOUTH MENTOR.

IN 2021, HE LAUNCHED THE CHATTANOOGA FIRE DEPARTMENT READ TO SUCCEED LITERACY PROGRAM AT HIS FORMER ELEMENTARY SCHOOL. ALLEN IDENTIFIED A CRITICAL NEED TO IGNITE A PASSION FOR READING AMONG STUDENTS TO IMPROVE LITERACY RATES. THE PROGRAM AIMED TO BUILD POSITIVE CONNECTIONS BETWEEN STUDENTS AND FIREFIGHTERS, ENHANCE LITERACY LEVELS, AND INTRODUCE YOUNG LEARNERS TO THE FIRE SERVICE THROUGH LITERATURE. AS HE INTERACTED WITH MORE STUDENTS AND EXPLORED VARIOUS BOOKS, HE RECOGNIZED THE NEED TO WRITE HIS OWN BOOK TO CONVEY ESSENTIAL FIRE AND LIFE SAFETY MESSAGES EFFECTIVELY TO HIS YOUNG AUDIENCE. HIS GENUINE PASSION IS ROOTED IN EDUCATION AND COMMUNITY OUTREACH.

ALLEN IS A PROUD RECIPIENT OF THE 2019 AMERICAN RED CROSS HEROES AWARD FOR SERVICE TO YOUTH, AND HE WAS HONORED AS THE 2023 TENNESSEE PUBLIC FIRE EDUCATORS ASSOCIATION PUBLIC FIRE EDUCATOR OF THE YEAR. ADDITIONALLY, HE RECEIVED THE 2023 BETHLEHEM CENTER EDUCATIONAL CHAMPION AWARD.

## SOLUTION FOR HELP JACOB FIND HIS WAY TO THE MAILBOX!!

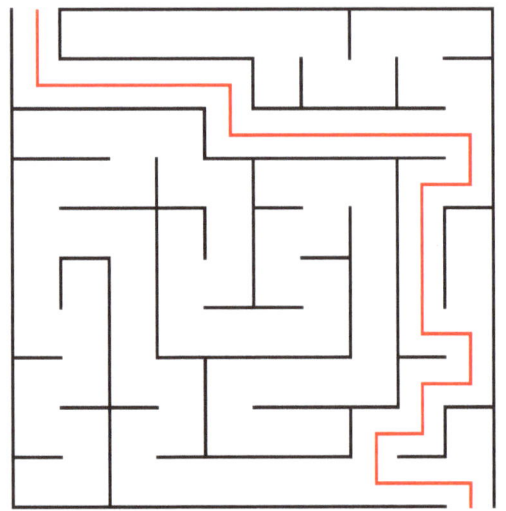

## SOLUTION FOR HELP THE FIRETRUCK SAVE THE BURNING HOUSE!

## SOLUTION FOR WORD SEARCH

www.ingramcontent.com/pod-product-compliance
Lightning Source LLC
Chambersburg PA
CBHW060800090426
42736CB00002B/95